Companion in Faith

The Power of Forgiveness

Patrice Fagnant-MacArthur

Our Sunday Visitor
Huntington, Indiana

24 23 22 21 20 19 1 2 3 4 5 6 7 8 9

Our Sunday Visitor Publishing Division
Our Sunday Visitor, Inc.
200 Noll Plaza
Huntington, IN 46750
www.osv.com
1-800-348-2440

ISBN: 978-1-68192-466-3 (Inventory No. T2349)
LCCN: 2019940330

Cover design: Tyler Ottinger
Cover art: Shutterstock.com
Interior design: Lindsey Riesen

PRINTED IN THE UNITED STATES OF AMERICA

Introduction

"Forgive us our trespasses as we forgive those who trespass against us." How many times have we uttered those words in the Lord's Prayer? Probably hundreds, if not thousands. But how many times have we stopped to consider what we are saying? We are asking God, whom we have hurt with our sins, to treat us the same way we treat those who have hurt us. Do we really mean that?

It is hard to ask for forgiveness. It is difficult to admit that we have done wrong, that we have failed in our relationships with God and with others. This is one reason people shy away from the Sacrament of Reconciliation. It is very humbling to have to name our failings out loud to another person. The bigger the failing, the more humbling it is. And yet God's mercy is always there. The grace flowing through the sacrament as the priest utters the words of absolution is very powerful. The knowledge that we are forgiven can lift the weight of the world off our shoulders. More than once, I've left the confessional with tears of joy and relief streaming down my face.

As hard as it is to get in line for the Sacrament of Reconciliation and to admit our sins out loud to God in the person of the priest, it can be even harder to forgive those who have harmed us. The bigger the hurt, the bigger the challenge it is to extend mercy. Some wounds just don't heal. Sometimes, we don't want to forgive. Instead, we want to hold on to that anger and hurt because it gives us a sense of control over the situation. We feel righteous in our anger: We were right and the other person was wrong.

Yet the cost of holding on to bitterness and not forgiving is huge. Fr. Carlos Martins, CC, offers this perspective: "While refusing to forgive has appeal in terms of the power and energy that bitterness *appears* to offer, in the end it merely leaves us stuck in a cycle of perpetual loss and distress and holds us in permanent victimhood. Indeed, for a person to not forgive is equivalent to his drinking poison, but desiring someone else to die of it. It is completely irrational."[1]

It is important to caution that extending forgiveness does not mean willingly subjecting ourselves to continuing abuse. We are called to love and forgive others, but we are also called to love ourselves. There are times when we must remove ourselves from unsafe situations. However, even in these difficult circumstances, we are still called to forgive.

God's mercy and forgiveness are immeasurable and always there for the asking. But the prayer that Jesus taught us clearly says that God will forgive us as we forgive others. This means that we need to extend mercy to others if we want God to forgive us. The prayers and reflections in this devotional focus on the challenge and power of offering forgiveness. Through the grace of God, may the process of forgiving bring healing both to ourselves and to those who have hurt us.

A Young Girl Models Forgiveness

"Looking back at my past, I can see that in my youth, I chose a bad path, which led me to ruin myself. … Maria Goretti, now a saint, was my good angel, sent to me from God to guide and save me. She prayed for me, she interceded for me, her murderer."

— Alessandro Serenelli

Maria Goretti was not yet twelve years old when Alessandro Serenelli, a farmworker who lived with the Goretti family in Nettuno, Italy, stabbed her to death for refusing his sexual advances. Despite having been stabbed fourteen times, Maria briefly survived the brutal attack, suffering in the hospital for twenty hours before succumbing to her injuries on July 6, 1902. During that time, she stated repeatedly that she forgave her attacker.

Alessandro, however, was unrepentant. Then, during his third year in prison, Maria appeared to him in a dream. She smiled and offered him fourteen flowers — one for each stab wound; he felt a great sense of peace and experienced a profound conversion. When he was released after twenty-seven years in prison, his first act was to go to Maria's mother, Assunta Goretti, to beg for her forgiveness. Assunta told him: "Maria has forgiven you, and surely God has forgiven you. Who am I to withhold my forgiveness?"

Prayer

Saint Maria Goretti, please help me to follow your example of willingness to forgive.

Reflection

The first step in forgiving is to acknowledge the pain that the other person has caused you. What hurts in your life are you holding on to? Whom do you struggle to forgive?

What Does It Mean to Forgive?

"Be kind to one another, tenderhearted, forgiving one another, as God in Christ forgave you."

— Ephesians 4:32

What does it mean to forgive? Does it mean that we pretend that the wrong was never committed? While that might work for small offenses, it isn't practical or advisable for large ones. We can't simply forget that someone murdered or maimed a loved one or that someone abused us or stole something of great value from us. The wounds from such actions are real and long-lasting. And it is prudent to do what we can to protect ourselves and others from further harm from these individuals.

So what does forgiveness look like in such cases of grave harm? It looks like this: We acknowledge that the wrong can never be made right by the person who caused it; then we turn over all our anger and pain and desire for revenge to God. Doing so will not heal us suddenly. In fact, we may have to turn the situation over to God repeatedly.

Forgiveness, like love, is much more of an action than a feeling. Just as we can make a choice to love, to wish what is good for a person even when we don't feel like it, we can make the choice to let go of our anger and hurt even when the feelings run deep. The decision to forgive comes first. The feelings will follow in time.

Prayer

Dear God, help me to make the decision to forgive even when I don't feel like forgiving.

Reflection

What anger and resentment are you holding on to? Turn those feelings over to God. Tell God that you are making the decision to forgive and let go of your hurt.

They Know Not What They Do

"And Jesus said, 'Father, forgive them; for they know not what they do.'"

— Luke 23:34

Jesus forgave not only those who personally ordered and carried out his torture and crucifixion, but all those who contributed by standing in the crowd shouting, "Crucify him!" When we repeat these words on Palm Sunday and Good Friday, we are forced to think about our role in crucifying Jesus.

When I sin, I'm not consciously trying to hurt Jesus. Instead, I'm thinking about what seems good for me in that moment. The devil is skilled at making what is evil seem attractive, and my human nature is weak. The guilt comes later, after I've given in to temptation.

The same holds true for people who sin

against us. Very rarely are people intentionally trying to ruin our lives or inflict long-lasting emotional pain. Instead, they are giving in to their human weakness: They are tired, frustrated, or angry about the pain in their own lives and take out their rage on us. Their decision-making is often hampered by addiction or by mental illness. The sins are real; the pain they cause is real — but they know not what they do.

Prayer

Dear Jesus, help me to forgive those who hurt me due to their human weakness, just as you forgive all humanity, whose sins wound you.

Reflection

Looking over your life, can you recall times when you unintentionally deeply hurt someone else due to your human weakness? Consider those who have hurt you. What human weaknesses were they battling?

Pray for Those Who Mistreat You

"'But I say to you that hear, Love your enemies, do good to those who hate you, bless those who curse you, pray for those who abuse you.'"

— Luke 6:27–28

These teachings of Jesus are some of the most challenging words in all of Scripture. *Love your enemies*! Our natural inclination is not to want what is good for our enemies; we want their lives to be horrible. When someone hates us, we tend to respond with hate.

Jesus asks us to want what God wants even for those who have hurt us. But on our own, we can't overcome our human tendency to meet a negative emotion with an equally negative emotion. We need God's help. This is where prayer comes in.

We can pray for our enemies. Praying for

someone daily, asking God to bless that person and help that person to be all that God wants him or her to be, will transform our feelings toward the person. While this change will likely not happen overnight, it will happen. You can't hate someone you pray for on a regular basis. While you may need to remove yourself from an abusive or dangerous situation, you can continue to pray for the person who has hurt you. And God may respond to your intercession for your "enemy" by healing that person's heart along with your own.

Prayer

Dear Jesus, please bless my enemies. Please help them be who you want them to be.

Reflection

Who are your enemies? How do you feel about them? Can you commit to praying for these people on a daily basis?

Leave the Judging to God

"Judge not, and you will not be judged; condemn not, and you will not be condemned; forgive, and you will be forgiven."

— Luke 6:37

There are objective moral wrongs in the world, and Jesus calls us to judge and speak out against what is sinful. What we cannot judge is the person who is sinning, even when that person has caused us harm. The Vatican II document *Gaudium et Spes* makes this distinction clear:

> It is necessary to distinguish between error, which always merits repudiation, and the person in error, who never loses the dignity of being a person even when he is flawed by false or inadequate religious notions. God alone

> is the judge and searcher of hearts, for that reason He forbids us to make judgments about the internal guilt of anyone.[2]

We are called to hate the sin but love the sinner. When we struggle to forgive those who have sinned against us, we must remember that we are all sinners in need of God's mercy. Because we cannot know what is going on in someone's heart, we cannot make judgments about the state of any person's soul. Only God sees everything inside of us: the circumstances that have led us to where we are today, the pain we have suffered, our inherent human weaknesses, and the motivation for our actions. Forgiveness without judgment does not mean we pretend the wrong did not happen. It does mean that we cannot judge the motives of the person who did the wrong. We are called to pray for that person, to speak the truth in love and kindness, to forgive the person for any harm they have caused us, and to leave the rest to God.

Prayer

Dear God, please help me to remember that you, and only you, are the judge of human hearts. Please help me to speak against sin but always strive to love the sinner.

Reflection

Is there anyone in your life that you have been judging harshly? The next time you are tempted to condemn someone, stop to pray first for wisdom and understanding. Is there a way you can condemn the sin while still loving and forgiving the person?

A Priest in Auschwitz Forgives

"We go to the glory of the Resurrection by way of suffering and the Cross."
— Saint Maximilian Kolbe

Maximilian Kolbe was a Franciscan priest in the 1930s in Poland, where he published a Catholic newspaper and magazine, started a radio station, and founded a monastery. During World War II, the friars hid thousands of Polish and Jewish refugees.

The German Gestapo arrested Father Kolbe, sending him first to a prison in Pawiak and then to Auschwitz. While in the concentration camp, Father Kolbe urged his fellow prisoners to forgive their captors and to meet evil with good.

In July 1941, a prisoner from Father Kolbe's barracks disappeared. The deputy camp commander ordered his officers to choose ten men from the same barracks to be starved to death as punishment for the escape and as a deterrent to further escape attempts. One of the men chosen protested that he had a family. Father Kolbe offered to take his place, and his offer was accepted. He comforted the dying men, leading them in songs and prayers each day. After two weeks, the four men left alive were killed by injection with carbolic acid. Father Kolbe willingly offered his arm for the injection and prayed for the man administering the lethal dose. The prisoner Father Kolbe had saved was present at Father Kolbe's canonization in 1982.

Prayer

Saint Maximilian Kolbe, please help me to imitate your willingness to love and forgive without counting the cost.

Reflection

What is the worst thing that someone has ever done to you or a loved one? How did you respond? Today, offer a prayer for the person or persons who hurt you.

Wipe the Slate Clean

"Then Peter came up and said to him, 'Lord, how often shall my brother sin against me, and I forgive him? As many as seven times?' Jesus said to him, 'I do not say to you seven times, but seventy times seven.'"

— Matthew 18:21–22

In the Hebrew Scriptures, seven is considered the number of completeness and perfection. Thus, when Peter asks if he should forgive seven times, he is not being stingy. Yet Jesus rejects his proposal and expands the perfect number exponentially. Jesus is essentially telling us that we are not to keep count of sins committed against us; we are not to maintain a ledger of past wrongs.

People who are in close relationship with each other frequently keep a record of past wrongs. Someone makes a mistake, and instead of addressing that mistake, we start in on a litany of all the other mistakes he or she has made in the past. Phrases like "You always … " and "How many times have I told you … " come out of our mouths. Instead of forgiving past wrongs and wiping the slate clean, we leave every mark on it until the slate is such a dirty mess that we can see nothing but wrongs.

Imagine if God dealt with us this way. I know when I go to confession, I tend to have to list the same sins over and over — I keep trying to do better but inevitably fail. What if when we asked for forgiveness, God instead brought up everything we had ever done wrong in our lives? What a pile of sin that would be! We would be buried under it. Thankfully, God forgets our sins while he is forgiving them (cf. Hebrews 8:12). God wants us to treat our loved ones with the same generous forgiveness (and forgetfulness) he extends to us.

Prayer

Dear God, please help me to stop keeping a record of wrongs. Please help me to forgive others as you forgive me.

Reflection

What are some wrong things that you do over and over again? Are there things your loved ones do that offend you over and over again? Do you keep track of all these offenses?

The Radical Forgiveness of the Father

"Let us eat and make merry; for this my son was dead, and is alive again; he was lost, and is found."

— Luke 15:23b–24

The parable of the prodigal son (cf. Luke 15:11–32) is one in which we may relate to different characters at different times in our lives. Sometimes we are the repentant child returning to God after a time away, begging for forgiveness. Sometimes we are the older brother, resentful and jealous. And then there are the times when God calls us to imitate him and be the one who forgives.

The father in this story practices radical forgiveness. The son comes back humbled. He had rejected his family and knows that he has no reason to expect a warm welcome. He's willing to be a servant. His father could have forgiven him and taken him back as a servant instead of a son; by human reasoning, he would have been perfectly justified. How many times do we do this? We "forgive" someone but then continue to treat them as *persona non grata*. We exclude them from social events. We whisper about them behind their backs. We never let them forget that they did something wrong. Yet this is not what the father does.

Instead, the father runs enthusiastically out to the returning son and welcomes him home with open arms. He restores his wayward son to his original position in the family and throws a feast for him.

Prayer

Dear God, please help me to follow your example of welcoming and fully forgiving the sinner who repents.

Reflection

Is there someone in your life who wronged you in some way, whom you now treat as a second-class citizen? How can you be more like the father in the parable of the prodigal son?

God Can Use Everything for Our Good

"We know that in everything God works for good with those who love him, who are called according to his purpose."
— Romans 8:28

One of the greatest examples of this New Testament quote in action is the story of Joseph as told in the Hebrew Scriptures. Joseph is the eleventh son of Jacob, who makes no secret of the fact that Joseph is his favorite. Joseph's older ten brothers therefore resent him, and their antipathy only grows when Joseph taunts them by describing to them his dreams of his own greatness and their subservience to him. Fed up with the young upstart, his brothers sell Joseph into slavery and tell their father that the boy has been killed by a wild animal.

His captors take Joseph to Egypt and sell

him to Potiphar, one of Pharaoh's officers. He earns great favor with his master. However, when Joseph rejects the advances of Potiphar's wife, she lies about him, and Joseph ends up in prison. Fortunately, the prison keeper befriends Joseph and learns of his ability to interpret dreams. When Joseph is able to interpret Pharaoh's dreams, Pharaoh rewards him with a position of honor overseeing the lands of Egypt. This puts him in a position of power over his brothers when they come to Egypt to beg for food during a time of great famine.

Instead of using his power to deny them the food they and their families so desperately need, Joseph forgives his brothers, telling them, "You meant evil against me; but God meant it for good, to bring it about that many people should be kept alive, as they are today" (Gn 50:20). God is always working in our lives, even when it seems that he is absent. He can bring light out of our darkest days, and his care for us makes it possible for us to extend forgiveness rather than revenge.

Prayer

Dear God, I can't always see you working in my life. Please help me always to trust that you can bring good out of evil.

Reflection

Do you struggle with trusting in God's goodness? Do you feel that the dark hours of your life are the end of the story? Do you feel that you must right wrongs through retaliation rather than forgiveness? Write down the above verse from Romans, and put it somewhere where you will see it regularly.

A Former Slave Forgives Her Captors

"If I were to meet the slave-traders who kidnapped me and even those who tortured me, I would kneel and kiss their hands, for if that did not happen, I would not be a Christian and religious today."

— Saint Josephine Bakhita

Josephine Bakhita was born in Darfur (now in western Sudan) in 1869. Her uncle was a tribal chief, and she had a happy childhood. But her happiness met a cruel end when she was captured by Arab slave traders at the age of nine and forced to walk barefoot 600 miles to southern Sudan. Over the course of twelve years, she would be bought, sold, and given away several times.

At one point, she was owned by a Turkish general, whose wife branded her, cutting into her with a razor and then rubbing salt into the wounds to ensure that they would scar. She was left with over 100 such brandings on her breasts, torso, and arms. She also experienced cruel beatings. One time she was beaten so severely that she couldn't function for a month.

In 1888, her Italian owner left her with the Canossian Sisters in Venice. The sisters taught her about God, and she ultimately decided to join the order. She received her sacraments of initiation from the future Pope Pius X in 1890 and made her final religious vows in 1896. As a sister, she worked as a doorkeeper and cook at the convent. She also helped prepare other sisters to go to work in Africa. She died in 1947 and was canonized by Pope Saint John Paul II in 2000.

Saint Josephine Bakhita suffered incredible horrors, yet she was deeply grateful to the slave traders because the road they put her on led her to God. That's true forgiveness.

Prayer

Saint Josephine Bakhita, please help me to follow your example of seeing the good that God can bring out of evil and pain. Pray for me to have the grace to forgive even the worst offenses, trusting that God is working all things for my good.

Reflection

Think of an injustice committed against you. Did any good ultimately come out of it? Does acknowledging the good make it easier to forgive the wrongdoing? Do you believe that God can bring good out of your pain? Why or why not?

Relieve a Heart That Is in Misery

"Blessed are the merciful, for they shall obtain mercy."

— Matthew 5:7

If we want to receive mercy, we must show it. Is mercy the same as forgiveness? No. Forgiveness can be part of mercy, but mercy goes beyond forgiveness. The Latin word for mercy is *misericordia,* which is "derived from the two words *miserere* ('pity' or 'misery') and *cor* ('heart'). … [W]hen we ask for God's mercy, we are essentially asking him to relieve us of a heart that is in misery."[3] By the same token, when we extend mercy to a person who has hurt us, we are helping to heal his or her heart.

Someone who hurts another person usually has a heart that is hurting. Often people hurt others because of the pain or abuse that was inflicted on them, and it becomes a vicious cycle. They may not realize the source of their own hurt. They may not even realize that what they did was wrong. If we respond with anger and return the hurt, we only add fuel to the fire. If we extend mercy, we can help break the cycle. In turn, God will extend mercy to us and help heal our own suffering hearts.

Prayer

Dear God, please help me to show mercy and heal the suffering hearts of those who have hurt me.

Reflection

When someone hurts you, do you ever think of the pain that person might have experienced or be experiencing? If you can't imagine forgiving what was done to you, can you envision playing a part in healing that person's broken heart? Can you trust that God will also help your heart to heal?

Choose Love

"Love is patient and kind; love is not jealous or boastful; it is not arrogant or rude. Love does not insist on its own way; it is not irritable or resentful; it does not rejoice at wrong, but rejoices in the right. Love bears all things, believes all things, hopes all things, endures all things. Love never ends."

— 1 Corinthians 13:4–8a

The people we love the most are also the people who have the most power to hurt us (and vice versa). They know all our weak points and what buttons to push to aggravate us or make us feel bad about ourselves. They know our past wrongs and failings. In times of stress or in the heat of an argument, they may stoop to throwing these painful memories in our face.

According to Saint Paul, those who love each other should never sink so low — love should never be ugly. But while we should all strive for Saint Paul's ideal of perfect love, the sad truth is that we are all sinners, and sometimes sin temporarily prevails.

How do we respond when someone we care about deeply causes us great pain? Do we hold on to the hurt, adding it to a mental list of everything our loved one has ever done to us? Do we replay the hurtful words or actions over and over in our head, becoming more angry and hurt with every replay? Saint Paul tells us that love is not resentful. Rather, love calls us to forgive our loved ones for the hurts they inflict on us, just as our loved ones are called to forgive us when we hurt them.

Prayer

Dear God, please give me the strength not to be resentful about the hurts my loved ones have caused me. Help me to choose love.

Reflection

Think of a time when you said something in anger to a loved one or made a decision that hurt a loved one deeply. When the anger cooled, how did you feel about what you had done? Did you apologize? Did your loved one respond with forgiveness or more anger? The next time a loved one causes you pain, remember how you wanted to be treated when the roles were reversed.

Work to Heal the Rifts in Your Family

"So if you are offering your gift at the altar, and there remember that your brother has something against you, leave your gift there before the altar and go; first be reconciled to your brother, and then come and offer your gift."

— Matthew 5:23–24

Family feuds can last for decades. Sometimes the people involved no longer remember what caused the rift. Angry words are said, people take sides, and silence and animosity ensue. Hardness of heart takes over. This response can be self-protective: we don't want to be hurt by those we love, so we put up walls around our heart.

Regardless of the initial reason, both sides involved bear responsibility for the continued brokenness of the relationship. This means that we have agency: We can try to heal the rift. We can choose to remove the walls around our heart brick by brick. We can admit our own part in the feud and apologize for our stubbornness. While we can't control how the other side responds, we can choose to reach out with love and forgiveness.

We can also pray for family members from whom we are estranged. As the *Catechism of the Catholic Church* reminds us: "It is not in our power not to feel or to forget an offense; but the heart that offers itself to the Holy Spirit turns injury into compassion and purifies the memory in transforming the hurt into intercession" (CCC 2843).

Prayer

Dear God, please heal the rifts in my family. Help me to be an instrument of your peace. Send me your Spirit to turn my hurt into compassion and intercession.

Reflection

Is there someone in your family whom you are estranged from? What step or steps can you take to help heal the rift?

Put Down Your Stones

"Let him who is without sin among you be the first to throw a stone at her."

— John 8:7

The sin of the woman caught in adultery was real; what she did was wrong. And Jesus held her accountable, forgiving her but telling her, *Do not sin again*. When someone sins, especially when they sin against us, we can acknowledge that they have done something wrong without condemning the person. Instead of throwing stones, we can set them free to make things right.

Yet often it is simpler for us to see people as either good or evil. Of course, we see ourselves as good! Those who agree with our viewpoint are also on the good side. On the other side are all those who see the world differently. We often decide they are evil without making any effort to understand their situation, their thinking, or the reasons for their actions. We may not pick up literal stones, but we use all the powers at our disposal to hurt and shame them.

Yet we are all sinners in need of God's mercy. We all need to repent and amend our lives. And God forgives us and provides us with opportunities to change our lives. We must extend this same mercy to others.

Prayer

Dear God, please help me to condemn the sin but not the sinner. Help me to want those who have hurt me to amend their lives, rather than choosing to see them only through the lens of their hurtful actions.

Reflection

Are there any groups of people that you consider "evil" due to beliefs they hold? Make the effort today to understand a viewpoint that differs from your own.

A Pope Practices What He Preaches

"Forgiveness is above all a personal choice, a decision of the heart to go against the natural instinct to pay back evil with evil."

— Pope Saint John Paul II

On May 13, 1981, Pope John Paul II was crossing St. Peter's Square when a man tried to assassinate him. Mehmet Ali Ağca fired four shots at the pope. Two hit his lower intestine, one hit his right arm, and the last hit his left index finger. John Paul II believed that our Blessed Mother saved his life, as the attempt was made on the anniversary of the first apparition of Our Lady of Fatima in 1917.

Ağca was captured and sentenced to life in prison. John Paul II visited him in 1983, and the two talked for over twenty minutes. The pope remarked, "I spoke to him as a brother whom

I have pardoned, and who has my complete trust." He also gave his would-be murderer a rosary and requested that Ağca be pardoned. The Italian president respected the pope's wishes; Ağca was released and sent to Turkey, where he completed an earlier sentence for murder. He was released in 2010. In 2014, shortly after the pope was canonized, Ağca laid two dozen white roses on Pope John Paul II's tomb.

Saint John Paul II not only preached forgiveness, he showed true forgiveness to one who had caused him great harm.

Prayer

Pope Saint John Paul II, thank you for your example of Christian forgiveness. Please help me when I find it hard to forgive.

Reflection

Do you think that those who have hurt you deserve your forgiveness? Do you deserve to be forgiven for the wrong you have done? Is forgiveness ever deserved, or is it always a gift freely given?

The Value of Listening

"If your brother sins against you, go and tell him his fault, between you and him alone. If he listens to you, you have gained your brother."

— Matthew 18:15

One of the key features of any relationship is communication. Breakdowns in a relationship are often due to miscommunication or a failure to listen — truly listen — to each other. All relationships have their low points. Someone does or says something, or fails to do or say something, and we feel hurt and then angry. We feel wronged and resentful and struggle to forgive the fault.

What if, instead of stewing in our own sense of being wronged, we sat down with the person and listened to his or her side of the story? Honest communication can be risky, making us feel uncomfortable and vulnerable. On the one hand, we might find out right away that the person is struggling with a difficult situation unrelated to us, and that his or her words or actions that hurt us were unintentional side effects of stress. We could find out that we entirely misheard or misinterpreted the person's words or actions. On the other hand, we could find that we hold more responsibility for the situation than we thought. We might discover that we need to ask for forgiveness ourselves.

Even if it turns out that we were wholly justified in our feelings, speaking with the person who hurt us will help us understand more fully the reasons behind the offensive behavior.

Prayer

Dear God, please help me to have the courage and take the time to listen to others.

Reflection

When was the last time you had a meaningful conversation with a loved one? Is there someone you are having a hard time putting up with? Make a point of setting up a time to truly listen to that person.

What If the Person Isn't Sorry?

"He does not retain his anger for ever
because he delights in mercy."

— Micah 7:18b

Sometimes, the person who has hurt us is not sorry for what they have done. Perhaps they cannot or will not see where they were wrong, or they refuse to be reconciled with us. In these situations, it can be incredibly painful to try to forgive. Yet forgiveness is not just for the other person — it is also for us. Withholding forgiveness, while it may seem easier, only hurts us in the long run.

Moreover, only God can see inside each person's heart and know if he or she is truly sorry. A person may not seem sorry for what he or she has done to us, but we cannot know the heart. Perhaps that person is actually deeply sorry but can't figure out a way to say the words, or maybe the person's actions are influenced by mental or physical illness or addiction.

If the person truly is not sorry and doesn't care how we feel, our anger isn't going to have any impact. Instead, our anger will only cause us continued heartache. In any event, even if we cannot forgive the person right now, God still requires us to love him or her. We don't have to interact with the person (sometimes it is prudent not to), but we do have to will that person's good. It's hard to do that if we haven't forgiven.

Prayer

Dear God, help me to forgive even those who aren't sorry. Help me to will the good of others even when I can't seem to forgive them.

Reflection

Is there someone in your life who has hurt you and has not asked for forgiveness? Can you forgive the person for what he or she has done? If not, what is it costing you to withhold forgiveness?

Comfort Those Subject to Public Punishment

"But if any one has caused pain, he has caused it not to me, but in some measure — not to put it too severely — to you all. For such a one this punishment by the majority is enough; so you should rather turn to forgive and comfort him, or he may be overwhelmed by excessive sorrow."

— 2 Corinthians 2:5–7

The court of public opinion is particularly vicious these days. Anything a person did or said at any point in his or her life is subject to scrutiny, exposure, and mass shaming across social media in a matter of minutes. There is no statute of limitations, no room for apologies, no place for acknowledgment that a person may have grown or changed, no forgiveness. And no one is safe. We are all at risk of being defined by the worst thing we have ever said or done.

How do we navigate this "call-out culture"? Do we readily share and retweet posts and memes even when we have no personal involvement in or knowledge of the situation? Do we maintain an attitude of superiority and righteous indignation toward those who have been pilloried? Do we add to an individual's pain even though our connection to the alleged sin is limited to soundbites from the media? Are we willing and eager to help destroy a person? Is this the way we would want to be treated if our worst deed were on display for the world to see?

What if we left the judgment to others and responded differently? What if we extended mercy and understanding, praising the good the person may have accomplished in his or her life instead of focusing only on the wrongdoing? What if we practiced radical forgiveness, extending love and mercy instead of condemnation?

Prayer

Dear God, please help me to forgive instead of rushing to condemn others.

Reflection

Do you use social media to build others up or to tear them down? Before you share online gossip, stop to think about how you would want to be treated if you were the one whose sins were on public display.

Forgive the Dead

Eternal rest grant unto them, O Lord, and let perpetual light shine upon them. May the souls of the faithful departed, through the mercy of God, rest in peace. Amen.

As part of the communion of saints, we are called to pray for the dead. Our prayers and sacrifices can assist those in purgatory in completing their purification sooner so that they may share in the glories of heaven.

Yet sometimes our feelings toward a person who has died are complicated. We may not have forgiven the person while he or she was alive for some wrong committed against us — the person may have died unexpectedly, or we may simply not have been ready to forgive. Perhaps the person never expressed sorrow for what he or she did to us. Perhaps our pain was too deep. In the worst-case scenario, if it seems as though the wound inflicted on our soul will never heal, we may hope that the person went to hell.

As with all such situations, it is best to give our feelings to God. He knows how we feel and the reasons for those feelings. We can offer a prayer or request a Mass for the person even if we don't want to. In order for us to heal, we need to extend forgiveness. Otherwise, the anger and animosity will only fester inside of us.

Prayer

Dear God, you know the pain within my heart caused by my unforgiveness of those who are no longer here for me to speak to. I give all my hurt and anger to you.

Reflection

Are you struggling to forgive someone who has died? Write that person a letter expressing everything you wish you could say to them. After you are done, burn the letter or rip it in pieces. Then say a prayer for the person's soul, and have a Mass said for him or her.

The Challenge of Forgiving God

"My God, my God, why hast thou forsaken me? Why art thou so far from helping me, from the words of my groaning?"

— Psalm 22:1

What do we do when we are angry at God? We all question God's wisdom and care for us at one time or another: Our prayers have been ignored. Tragedy has befallen us. We are suffering, and God seems to have abandoned us. God's will (whether intentional or permissive) seems cruel.

First, as always, we can give our anger to God. He can take it. We can lash out and protest. The psalmist does it, as does the much-tortured figure of Job in the Old Testament. Job flat out tells God that it would have been better if he had never been born (cf. Jb 3). Yes, we can be angry with God.

Rabbis in Auschwitz put God on trial for the unspeakable pain and suffering that the Jewish people were experiencing. They found God guilty — and then went out to pray.[4] We can follow their example. We can show God all our anger, but in the end, we must remember that God is God and we are not. He is worthy of our worship and praise even when we feel abandoned. If we reject God, refusing to pray or go to church, we only hurt ourselves. As God told Job, "Where were you when I laid the foundation of the earth? … Shall a faultfinder contend with the Almighty? He who argues with God, let him answer it" (Jb 38:4a, 40:2).

God sees the whole picture of eternity; we see only a tiny portion. In the end, we must defer to his wisdom even when we do not understand it. Forgiving God really means surrendering to his wisdom and trusting in his providence, even when things do not make sense. There is no other answer.

Prayer

Dear God, help me always to remember that you

are God and I am not. Help me to trust in your goodness even when it feels as though you have abandoned me.

Reflection

Are you angry at God? Tell God about it. Give him all your rage and protests. Cry and scream if you need to. Let it out. Then, say a prayer of praise.

Sometimes the Person Hardest to Forgive Is Yourself

"'You shall love your neighbor as yourself.'"

— Mark 12:31

The commandment to love our neighbor presumes that we love ourselves. Yet all too often, we do not love ourselves. We treat ourselves badly for all sorts of reasons. Some reasons are fairly trivial (I've been known to hate myself for gaining weight), while others reach to the very core of our being. Often it is our sense of shame for our own sins or those that others have perpetrated against us that cause us to loathe ourselves.

Guilt can serve a good purpose. It is our conscience at work, letting us know that we have done something against God's law, breaking our relationship with God and/or others. Guilt can compel us to beg God for mercy and to ask others for forgiveness. It can bring us to our knees in the Sacrament of Reconciliation. But too often we struggle to leave behind the shame of our sins. We lay down our sin at the feet of Our Lord only to pick it back up as if we believe that our sins are too big for God to forgive.

Knowing we have done something horrible that we can't undo is a hard burden to carry. Even after God forgives us, we may face real-life consequences. And if we don't let go of the shame, it can make us hate ourselves. Yet, sometimes we hate ourselves for things that happened to us, abuse that we have suffered. We may blame ourselves for things that were out of our control. We may replay events, thinking that maybe we could have stopped them if only we had responded in a different way.

Self-hatred is not what God wants for us. God loves us and wants us to love ourselves. Jesus died on the cross for each one of us. This means that we need to extend to ourselves the same love and forgiveness we show to others.

Prayer

Dear God, please help me to love and forgive myself the way you love and forgive me.

Reflection

What shame do you carry with you? Do you ever suffer from self-hatred? If this is something you struggle with, please consult with a trusted priest, spiritual advisor, or counselor to get the help you need to love yourself the way God loves you.

Conclusion

Forgiveness is a powerful act. We can never merit God's forgiveness, yet he offers it to anyone who asks. God is always waiting with open arms to welcome us back home. But remember, the Lord's Prayer makes it clear that we must forgive if we want God to forgive us. Pope Francis acknowledges how difficult it is for us to forgive: "Forgiving the people who have offended us is not easy; it is a grace that we must ask for: 'Lord, teach me to forgive as you have forgiven me.' It is a grace. Through our own efforts we are unable: to forgive is a grace of the Holy Spirit."[5]

God calls us to forgive others, to share his love and mercy with all. With God's help, forgiving those who have hurt us will heal both our hearts and the hearts of others. Forgiveness can also heal relationships and divisions among peoples. Forgiveness has the power to change the world.

Notes

1. Fr. Carlos Martins, CC, "How to Forgive," accessed April 30, 2019, https://mariagoretti.com/how-to-forgive/.

2. *Gaudium et Spes*, 28. http://www.vatican.va/archive/hist_councils/ii_vatican_council/documents/vat-ii_const_19651207_gaudium-et-spes_en.html.

3. Jackie Francois-Angel, "What Does Mercy Mean?" DynamicCatholic.com, accessed April 30, 2019, https://dynamiccatholic.com/beautiful-mercy-program/reflections/what-does-mercy-mean.

4. Jenni Frazer, "Wiesel: Yes, We Really Did Put God on Trial," *The JC*, September 19, 2008, https://www.thejc.com/news/uk-news/wiesel-yes-we-really-did-put-god-on-trial-1.5056.

5. Pope Francis, General Audience of March 14, 2018, https://w2.vatican.va/content/francesco/en/audiences/2018/documents/papa-francesco_20180314_udienza-generale.html.

About the Author

Patrice Fagnant-MacArthur has a Master of Arts in Applied Theology. She is the author of *The Catholic Baby Name Book* and has contributed articles to several publications, including *Catechist*, *Today's Catholic Teacher*, *Baystate Parent*, *Seton Magazine*, *Publisher's Weekly*, *Catholic Library World*, and *Canticle*. A freelance Catholic writer and editor, she is also editor of TodaysCatholicHomeschooling.com. For more information, please visit pfmacarthur.com.